OUT OF BOUNDS

Dominique Hecq grew up in the French-speaking part of Belgium. She is the author of a novel (*The Book of Elsa*), three collections of short fiction (*Magic, Mythfits* and *Noisy Blood*), and three books of poetry (*The Gaze of Silence, Good Grief* and *Couchgrass*). Two of her one-act plays were performed in Australia, Belgium and Germany (*One Eye Too Many* and *Cakes & Pains*). Dominique's awards for poetry include The New England Review Prize for Poetry (2005) and The Martha Richardson Medal for Poetry (2006). She was also short-listed for the inaugural Blake Prize for Poetry (2008) and highly commended in its second year. She currently lives in Melbourne.

OUT OF BOUNDS

Dominique Hecq

re.press

PO Box 40, Prahran, 3181, Melbourne, Australia

http://www.re-press.org

© Dominique Hecq & re.press 2009

The moral rights of the authors have been asserted

Database right re.press (maker)

First published 2009

National Library of Australia Cataloguing-in-Publication Data
A catalogue record for this book is available from the National Library of Australia

Out of Bounds
Hecq, Dominique

ISBN: 978-0-9805440-3-9 (pbk)
ISBN: 978-0-9806665-3-3 (ebook)

Series: Anomaly

Designed and Typeset by A&R

Printed on-demand in Australia, the United Kingdom and the United States
This book is produced sustainably using plantation timber, and printed in
the destination market on demand reducing wastage and excess transport

OUT OF BOUNDS

Dominique Hecq

re.press

PO Box 40, Prahran, 3181, Melbourne, Australia

http://www.re-press.org

© Dominique Hecq & re.press 2009

The moral rights of the authors have been asserted

Database right re.press (maker)

First published 2009

National Library of Australia Cataloguing-in-Publication Data
A catalogue record for this book is available from the National Library of Australia

Out of Bounds
Hecq, Dominique

ISBN: 978-0-9805440-3-9 (pbk)
ISBN: 978-0-9806665-3-3 (ebook)

Series: Anomaly

Designed and Typeset by A&R

Printed on-demand in Australia, the United Kingdom and the United States
This book is produced sustainably using plantation timber, and printed in
the destination market on demand reducing wastage and excess transport

In the beginning was the word,
but was it followed by a question mark?

—Phyllis Webb

Acknowledgements

All of the pieces included here have been published before. My thanks go to Richard Hillman and The SideWaLK Collective for publishing 'The Gaze of Silence' as a slim volume, to Stephanie Holt for printing 'Out of Bounds' in *Meanjin* (June 1999), and to Michael Farrell for posting 'The Silence of the Gaze' on *Slope* (US) online. 'Out of Bounds' won the 1998 Melbourne Fringe Festival Prize for Outstanding Writing and Spoken Word Performance. With sincere thanks to Ali Alizadeh, Paul Ashton, Adam Bartlett and Justin Clemens. Thanks also to Noël Skrzypczak for the use of the cover image. As ever, my thanks are due also to Emmanuel, Jerome, Luke, Paul and Xavier Murphy. The extracts of works recited by the wild goat woman in 'The Gaze of Silence' are from Charles Baudelaire's 'The Seven Old Men', Virginia Woolf's *Three Guineas* and, with a twist, from J. S. Bach's *Mass in B minor*—The wild goat woman has in mind a recent recording with The Amsterdam Baroque Orchestra and Choir conducted by Ton Koopman. In 'The Silence of the Gaze' she quotes from 'The Seven Old Men' again, Shakespeare's *Macbeth*, Woolf's *Moments of Being* and Nietzsche's famous poem 'O Mensch' as sung in the fourth movement of Mahler's third symphony.

For Russell Grigg

Also by Dominique Hecq

Fiction—

>*The Book of Elsa*
>*Mythfits*
>*Magic & other stories*
>*Noisy Blood*

Poetry—

>*Good Grief*
>*Couchgrass*

Short Drama—

>*One Eye Too Many*
>*Cakes and Pains*

Contents

The Gaze of Silence

Any Thought utters a Dice Throw
—Stéphane Mallarmé

Incarnadine Sun

The skin of day bursts
A wild goat leaps off the page

Word *parola Wort mot woord*—
a dice throw cast in jest—
a tongue in free fall—
images adjust to words:
things said
things utterly written

Where do words come from?

From behind an eyelid
the world slows down
silence swaps
the living with the dead
the mother with the child
the dead for the living dead.

Is language the world?

Washed out Moon
     Milk letters spilled
  in mid air song

High up in the mountains she drops and falls in a mirror you call a lake. Her eyes are split and so is her face. Her skin is inside out. Burning. Freezing. She swims in air solid as glass, glimmering as silver. She wheels herself back through a field of rocks to what you would call home. She is all shivers and sweat. Her voice booms in her chest. Her head. Husks. Her heartbeat is strong. Is weak. Is no more. *How long must I wait for this death to come*, she asks—*for this death to go?* In a foreign tongue she hears that she is not prepared.

Hollowed out sky
Hooves crash
through the face of the world

In the mountains the sun is in need of light.
Mountain peaks flip back to river beds. She is out
of time. Out of space. Out of it. In it. In silence she
steps from silence to cadence. She feels for the beat.
She grabs words as though these are air bubbles
she needs to breathe. She says things like words to
speak death off. She is now. She was then. She will
be never. She is in jail. In a birth centre. In bedlam.
Lamb of Hades. A crowd gathers around her as sirens
toll for her tongue. Defaced bodies flicker past her.
Colours clash. Colours crash. She closes her eyes
with her own hand.

Sinking stars

Iceberg shadows

Diamonds of dew

She is and is not—counting faces at the back of the lake where she wants to jump. Where she wants to dream words that are not splinters under the skin but just grains of sand pressed into the paper. *Don't make a sound*, she tells him, *for your sounds swallow up my words, my only anchors in the world.* He sighs. He is a hawk-like man. He is a hawk. Red-eyed hawk. Red. He is aflame. Phoenix. *Son and father of himself.*

Rock clouds
A clutter of tongues
The gaze of silence

She is in limbo where blue is green is yellow is
white, where sweet is bland is bitter and bites, and
where silence is an incessant excess of violence.
For something to come about something must go away,
she hears. She wants to go. She wants to stay. As
in *bleiben* blubbering *blancheur des mots* blackness of
things blurring of boundaries bewitching soundaries
in Babel instead of that blundering *babbelchose* to
be—is a belle. She hangs on to the word word.

Air baubles
Bell bubbles
What's in a name?

Isabelle. Belle Is A French Sound meaning appealing
to the eye—the I of the *belholder*—in English belle
for a beautiful woman or *the* reigning beauty *of*
his place. Each language in its place. The romance
language of fear and the true language of romance.
Keep them separate for somewhere in between is the
spirit child, mother of poetry who will play the viola
d'armour with a ball of words to practice the viola
d'amore at the ball of worlds falling into words.

A crack in the night
Wild goat Ink
Sand life

She is in the sun, the one you call god. It is a
cold and quiet place. She is alone awaiting her
punishment for she made up the world when she
unveiled the word. Now all she knows is that it is
in silence and through silence only that one will
ever see the hidden one, that one will ever hear the
magic word and see it in the flesh. She wants to back
up, but she can't—not for all the copies of words of
love she has. She will try something new. He makes
a sound. There is no guilt. There are only words
-which is worse? She scratches her head and hears in
the future in her own voice—not her tongue; *It took
many years for me to realize I was not forgiven but given up
for being.*

Break of Light
A hand on a cheek
Paper love

From a dry lake she looks up. Her index finger
uncrosses her lips. She tells silence off—orders
it to squeeze its eyes shut. She tells tales of wild
mountain goats swimming, floating, wheeling across
rock waves, going up in smoke like the breath of
sand making mirrors, like the souls of sounds in
between words, like the souls of children sounding
in between homes not made of sandstone, like words
sounding, unsounding, resounding the world.

The secret of the wild

goat with a sliver of Sun in its eyes—
                                    Moonstruck Sun
is what she reads
        as the twilight cracks

                                        open
                            on a twyborn tale
            in the crossed out gaze
        sounding spaces in between
                                    here & beyond
                    inside outside
        worlds:
                        splinters under the skin
        grains of sand pressed into paper
things in between being & non being between
                        the apnoea & the breath
                the syncopation & the beat—
things short of words
                        where one feels
            one is not
                    enough
                    in the world.

High up in the mountains She looks in the mirror you call a lake. Now that she has been in the gaze of silence she looks silence in the eye. *As a woman, I have no country. As a woman I want no country*, she says, *but I have two homes—incarnadine words and incarnate worlds.* At that the silence of the gaze resonates with the music of the One, for out of some ill-extinguished hearth, the fear of poetry yields the poetry of fear.

And on earth peace to men and women of good will.

Out of Bounds

The sea has words that fuse and explode
when the earth listens
to her song resounding
in stone, wave after hour.

—José Emilio Pacheco

I seem to have lost the power of speech.

SPEECH: the sounding of a musical instrument; the action or the faculty of speaking.

SPEAKING: the ability to express thoughts or feelings by articulating sounds; the power to utter sentences—as in sententious, perhaps.

POWER: rule, authority, supremacy.

You seem to have lost the power of speech
says the man with a sneer.

He is smart.

I am dumb.

And so you write, he snarls.

I want to run.

He snorts.

I snap.

And so I run. Run away. From the wrath ringing.
Ringing back. Bringing back the smack. The lack.
I run backwards. Back to the wretch. The wreck
where whosoever raps the wind, runs the runaway,
wrings a tongue—

RINGS—

This is Viola. Viola Dali.

(Silence)

C'est la vie.

SPEECH: A SNARE
A SNARE WHOSE POWER IS
THE SENTENTIOUS SUPREMACY
SUPERSEDING MY SOLE ABILITY.

I am lost.
Speech lost me.
Out-s'lot-id me.
Me, sneak I'land.
The voice and the eyes and the eyes in the voice.
Devising lenses. Veering words—
devouring rows of vowels
riots of consonants
clicks of the tongue crystal clear.
Devoicing voice.
Vox the fox.

Lost your tongue? asked the man *farther* back.

(Silence).

Father Victor asking my name with Our Father
looking on
as I tripped
tripped in the crumpled hem of my frilly skirt
and ripped the holy picture of the Virgin Mary
and then daddy gripping me, crippling, stripping
giving me the strap
and strapping the child once pretty as a picture to the
bunk.

Holy Terror.

IS A BELLE

IS A BELLE

IS A BELLE

Perdu ta langue? asked the son of man on the cross.
(Silence).

The ways of God are unfathomable. *In nomine Patris...*
I passed out.

I took to the road.

The way was clear.

I, Viola *Délit* runawry running for the life of her.
Viola veiling violence evicting the voice running the vile fox on the run.

Time's running out.

I'll be writing.

Writing my way out in tongues.

HiER born hear dad HARE dead la did aah LIP lipping
away law did ha Ding-gong hand lapWing her.
M'elle borne la deed ah! Vie oh la...la voix ci lah dit ta!

Tullamarine, like aquamarine: *aqua mirabilis* of
creamy green passing into crystals of blue and yellow
and white, slowly turning solid.

I do not see that the green is grimy, that the blue is
grey and the yellow sallow, that the white is warm
ash like the powdery matter peeling off a dream put
to the test—ashes I do not toast but tuck away in
haste with other private refuse.

And past the portal I had pictured grand and
gleaming to mark the arrival of some new Viola to
this new is-land, I turn my eyes inward the other
Dali, for the sky whose colour matches the tacky
asphalt and concrete all around is too ominous for
me to face.

And so I run and hail a taxi.

The cab shoots through a makeshift landscape—not the land, the lush island, the harsh inland I had fathomed in my thoughts, but a dull and wayward sea of concrete and concreted paddocks. Padded land. And from this side of the contraflow lane, a padlocked land.

I do have all my faculties: there's been a crash and the taxi-driver read me not as a runaway with no luggage, but as a busy paying customer playing at being international.

Leaving as the luxury to abridge.
I left not because things were bad, but bland.
Blending and branding the breath of effigies in a
grand cavernous silence: the lap of devious masters of
sentences lisping holier than thou things with sounds
on the brink of the unsound.

I flew away.

I thought the sun would light a sea of fire between
here and there, would burn all of my letters, my
clothes, my books, my paintings, all that was left of
my music.

I could hear my crestfallen past crackle and sigh,
echo and die, in the waves ablaze.

I could see the clean sear of fire, the black flakes and
inky tongues torn free float upward, twist, turn and
gone.

Dramatic bonfire lit in mock *herternity. Veritas rei.*
Viola rites. Utter delirium *très* sense.

Perdu ta langue?
Cut off. Tucked away. Not lost.

M'elle born i am hell était itch threw litl'He & Id. Here
i'm ream make ink Vie Oh la blind to U glib nests end I
uptune to yore vowel-o-links.

I've got my new tongue tucked under my skin.
It won't scar.
I'm elated.

There are things I can't name yet, but I'll borrow
your words, your rules, your pens.

I'll perfect myself, my new pet self for you to pat.
Borrowed self on borrowed time.
Patter. Patter. Patter.

Time raining words aflame gone ashtray s'mothering
me into double speak.

I meet my other half.
My better half.
It doesn't hurt: I've *penfected* myself.
One is 'ailing smoothly in aquamarine waters.

The better half asks my hand.
Half way through the sentence I sense a *flew* bumps.
I put my hand to the lump in my throat.

I can now hear the thump of things unsaid, the
rumple and grumble of sounds echoing. I can feel
a rush of prickly things under my skin, like crystal
slivers all ruffled up and gushing through.

I expect to see a rash running all over that skin.
There is not the faintest blush. I laugh all things
sounding and resounding off my humpty half. I
laugh my hand off to Charles. With a no. With a yes.
I keep the write one.

Time burrows my soul raw.
Buries my raw soul as I borrow vowels and
consonants and silences to seal off the holes
between double speak and double entendre aboard
the *Holy Tamermony* my spouse translates as *je t'aime.*

I am abreast of the times on the Folly Road,
scattered abroad for ever and ever, *aman.*

Self-write E oust dit rage sore row fou lines Mund s'trap'y rêves wych qweep ring-in.

The sun runs the show here.

One protects one's body from head to toe.

I sheet mine in black.

One seeks the shade of the bush and shelters on the beach.

I try the shadows of the city.
I am with my better half of ten years, Charles
Moore, and what's left of our brood.
Swanston Walk.

Swans of stone walking, not talking.

Who was Swanston? I ask.

(Silence).

Stillness soundly defeating us.
Urban energy bashed awash on hot stone in stony air
ringing with silent notes.
Human energy bashed out. Washed away. Sunday.

Where are the people?

(Silence)

I look up.

I'm sure I can make the rugged writing in the sky speak.

Aletheia, it says in rune-like script with the voice of Our Father who cannot possibly be in hell spelling out *Lethe* just for me.

I can feel the towering heat and towering noise and towering stone twisting me upward, closing in.

I want to jump.

I turn my eyes away.

I jolt inside.

I am a ghost.

Ghostly jumpy mummy hosting chaotic echoes. Viola, disembodied body, numb instrument bombing memory. Booming naught. Unarticulated disarticulated scream. Naughty vox. Fox running to earth. At sea.

I am surprised to feel my child snuggle up to me.

I try to say something—I manage a quick hug and a wink.

Charles is way ahead.

Time to catch up.

I make it a rule to look at things through his eyes.
He is a photographer, a man of images and distance
a man with a trained gaze.
I try to position myself at a remove to fix this
disturbing migration of sensations I can't name on a
screen I could read—
a serial, sequenced, timed, coloured and illuminated
projection of images that speak without words.
For a split second I am a slide projector shuttling
History between apertures and time frames.

Speed skaters racing time around the concreted
corner of colonial art bombed in front of the State
Library remind me that our runways are really no-
through roads and us anachronistic signs on the
plane of History

History with a capital H, as in Humanity, not
humaneness, the capital letter that shuts out history
and herstory and stories about them. H Oz Bomb.

We are creatures bound to letters that thrive on
myths and rule out the authority of speech.
Lethal links on live listings.
Barbed wire litter.
There must be a way through.
A way within the bounds of possibility.
Moore. Now I think of the name a lot. It overrules
my story. Moore rhymes with more, the rime of
mort.

Mort à Letheia. Morte Dali. La-di-da. La violenca e
muerte. Law deed Rraah! Viola dead.

My death, the impossible. The impossible beyond the rattle of *maestros*, the necrophilic prattle.

Chante, alors, Viola! Sing, petit singe, petty sin!

I'd have to be a bow afire and singe those strings,
those highly strung strings that strap me to the holy
instrument I profane across tongues.

We walk and walk rood after rood, not hand in
hand, but at arm's length, for bodies don't touch in
this armchair land of adventure lovers on screen.

As I finger my mooring armband it strikes me that
what's left of my ringed hand is numb.
Pace.

SPEECH-less: TONGUE-TIED INTO RASH
RESISTANCE; MY DESISTENCE; OUR
SENTENCE.

I must touch.

I must run my fingers on this rueful body, run
them on the skirt of scar tissue, uncrumple it, run a
tacking thread though it, not tuck it in. I must feel
the wind.

I must speak.

Speak lest the crack in the fake hearing aid we stick
onto speech acts called communication crackles and
kills us through the sheer power of make-believe.

I can hear them now running to and fro, to and fro,
at the M.C.G., where Australia hits the mark time
after time on the screen. Fifteen Love. Thirty Love.

Anybody home? I hear in the distance of my own
din.
(Silence)
Anybody in he-eare? tugs my child at my elbow.
She's lost the power of speech, I hear the man, my
man,   sneer.

Love. *Vole, Viola. Vole!*

Look!

Look. Don't run. Unhaste time.

SPEECH AS SPARE THREAD IN THE
BOW WHOSE POWER IS TO TACK IN,
TACK THROUGH, THE SET OF STRINGS
ANCHORING MY WHOLE ABILITY—TO BE.

The wind wraps around my body.
I clasp my instrument and score:

Sorry, love, what is it?

The Silence of the Gaze

The prolonged wound-consciousness after the
bullet's shot
The love after the look is dead,
the yellow joy after the song of the sun.

—Muriel Rukeyser

Incarnadine Moon
The body of night bleeds
Wild goat woman falls off the Book

Dreams collect images collect words
from the glaze of eyes
that shoot silence through the mouth—
       things not said
    things mute unwritten

Where do thoughts come from?

From behind an eyeball
words gather
the dust of images:
worlds
known to the living in the dead
the mother in the child
the mute in the living dead.

Is thinking sleeptalking?

Sunlit Moon
Dream flesh
Skin of dawn

Down below in the city where wild goats turn
into demons she walks. Around the corner from St
Francis she meets red-eyed Charles. *Is this the city full
of dreams, where the spectre in broad daylight accosts the
passer-by?* he asks. She looks into his eyes and hears
echoes of words by a Phoenix less sinister than wise.
She shrugs her shoulders and slips her hands in her
pockets. She makes tracks. She is all ears. She will
keep her eyes peeled.

Full bellied Sun
Breeze hush
Blank-eyed world

Down little Lonsdale at noon she bumps into a
bearded old man, his spine *forming a perfect right
angle with his legs*. Pauper? Prophet? Patriarch? Poet?
He looks into her eyes & she shivers. Behind him
six more identical shapes follow. Hellish crescendo
of condemning silences. Cacophonous cortège of
gazing spectres. She will not freak out. She will not
run home and lock the door. She turns a blind eye to
this company of cackling spooks. She looks the old
man in the eye.

Southerly smack
Glitter sails
Veined city streets

In the old man's eyes she sees not a gaze, but a
monstrous sea ablaze. She sees men with feet of clay
clad like priests and patriarchs and prosecutors—not
prophets. She sees that she is a woman about to fall
into the abyss of one gaze. Her Own Abyss. *This my
hand will rather The multidinous seas incarnadine, Making
the green one red*, she hears. Now she knows that hers
is not a shoreless sea. She turns around. She will
follow the veined city street uphill.

Marble clouds
A clatter of tongues
The silence of the gaze

She is in once upon a time where questions are
just mortal, not lethal. Where the *AHRrr, haven't
I got you now?* is never followed by *You don't have a
Clear Conscience?* Where each reflection of yourself
in the mirror doesn't force you to revise the whole
universe. Where the mind doesn't poke its head out
at every step you take, flinging its ancestral fear in
your face, repeating again and again that if you trip
One will lock you up in once a pun at a time that
gives meaning to your name, for the One is just an
excuse for lonesome still-lives.

Bulbous eye of day
   Wild goat blood
   Rock fear

GET REAL, she reads on the wall of a nightclub or bar, *JOIN NEIGHBORHOOD WATCH*. She is in the world, of course, where dogs leave their mark on the threshold of churches, where diggers excavate the veined alleys awash with the sweat of women, where prisons are turned into museums and museums into prisons. She is in the world where she can shake the shackles of some *mythcarried* chance off her shoulders just as she can change the spelling of neighbor—Yes! if she says *objectified chance* right now, fear becomes just a word. Babel, a world puffed away.

Griffon wings
A claw in the mouth
Scream page

In the distance sirens toll for a life, a black shape
merging with the black of Spring street buildings
and post-politics, merging with the blood drying
in the open mouth of a tongueless child—*dream
addhimct, dipshermaniac, dopeher, junkhe, drug bindher,
world dealher, word leadher.* Post old thing. Ding Dong
Bells. Black-lipped spirit child—mother of poetry
Is A Belle. She is on her way, walk-writing the city
with wild goat ink blending the dust in her veins,
silencing the gaze.

The secret of the wise

woman with yellow Moons for eyes—
Sunstruck Moons
is what she writes
as the twilight clamps
shut
on a twyborn tale
out of the crossed out gaze
fleshing spaces in between
here & beyond
inside   outside
words—
splinters out of the skin
specks of sun squeezed out of paper
things from between being & non being
between
the apnoea & the breath
the syncopation & the beat—
things short of worlds
where one feels
One is enough
through the WORlD.

High up in Spring street in the city she stands
waiting for the tram. *Certainly and emphatically there
is no God; we are the words; we are the music; we are the
thing itself,* she tells the man with a golden cross in his
lapel and a violin case under his arm who looks her
in the eye. The man shrugs his shoulders and moves
on. She smiles at a woman who joins her in the
queue. *Isn't silence a raucous thing?* she asks. A glance
of acquiescence is all she demands. But the woman
has her own tale to tell. It begins with the image of a
wild goat leaping off the edge. It ends in song—

aus tiefen Traum bin ich erwacht:—
(from a deep dream I have awoken)

www.ingramcontent.com/pod-product-compliance
Lightning Source LLC
Chambersburg PA
CBHW031004090426
42737CB00008B/678